Copyright © 2024 by Matteo Bonistalli

All rights reserved.

All rights reserved. No part of this book may be reproduced, stored in a retrieval system or transmitted in any form or by any means, electronic, mechanical, photocopying, recording or otherwise, without the written authorisation of the author.

The limited use of quotations or extracts from the work for academic or critical purposes is permitted, provided that the author's name and the source of the work are indicated.

Translated by *Beatrice Giacometti*

Matteo Bonistalli

Beyond Leadership

Considerations on the Challenges of Implementing Modern Management Strategies

Table of Contents

Foreword of Fulvio Palmieri — 7

Introduction to the following Book — 11

Awareness about Our Social Culture — 15

The Cultural Influence on Leadership Selection — 25

Leader Development and Leadership: An Individual Commitment to Achieving a Collective Goal — 37

Employees: An Active Part in Leadership Dynamics — 53

The Perception of Surrounding Reality: Deception or Lack of Information? — 63

Communication: The Starting Point to change the Narrative of the surrounding World — 79

Bibliography — 101

Foreword

The theme of leadership not only permeates the fabric of the contemporary working world but also challenges the educational and training structures that prepare new generations of leaders. In a period of incessant and often radical transformations, the figure of the leader, the ways in which they exert their influence on organizations and individuals, and the system that shapes their competencies deserve thorough critical examination. Through the pages of this book, Matteo Bonistalli offers a sharp and often provocative reflection on these complex themes.

Matteo invites readers to critically reflect on how leadership training is implemented and how it can sometimes perpetuate outdated practices rather than innovate and adapt to the needs of the modern world. He poses essential questions: Are current training methodologies truly effective in preparing leaders to foster well-being and growth within organizations? Or do these methodologies tend to reinforce antiquated models, incapable of supporting a context that demands flexibility, empathy, and the ability to innovate?

With a style that balances accessibility and academic rigor, Matteo explores not only the qualities traditionally attributed to effective leaders but also how these qualities are taught. He criticizes the often static and theoretical approach to leadership training, suggesting that true change requires a more dynamic and personalized approach capable of addressing today's challenges.

This book does not limit itself to criticism; it also aims to inspire. It offers new perspectives on how leadership and the training system can be rethought to provide more adequate responses to the complex dynamics of our time.

Targeting a broad audience, from university students and organizational theorists to experienced managers and human resources professionals, every reader will find in these pages both food for critical thought and prompts for reflective action.

As you read, I encourage you to consider not only how the theories presented apply to leaders in high-level positions but also how each of us, through our daily interactions, can exercise a form of leadership. I hope that the following pages will serve not only as a critique but also as an invitation to action for positive change, with the hope that every leader can become a promoter of well-being and innovation.

Fulvio Palmieri

Founder @ RisorseUmane-HR.it |
Online Growth Advisor |
HR Services Consultant

Chapter 1
Introduction to the following Book

For those who approach the reading of this book, I wish to highlight immediately that you will not find specific strategies or innovative theories to apply to the world of *work*: despite some due references to recalled theories, everything will turn around my point of *observation*, focusing my attention on aspects related to the problems that characterize this environment and that others have already brought to light from their own perspective.

Obviously, since I can't define myself as either a *philosopher* or a *scientist* capable of endorsing or criticizing theories, researches, and experiments - which nonetheless have a specific value in the context in which they were introduced and used - my attempt is to make those people interested in employment and human resources reflect on the topics I address, by lending those who undertake this reading the *lenses* with which I am observing this specific world: it is often by looking from a different angle that one discovers beauties ignored by many.

Aside from principles, all sciences, especially those dealing with the most intrinsic aspects of the human being, never achieve *absolutely* accurate or *infinitely* valid results, as they depend on the knowledge and resources available to scientists at the time of their discovery. To give a simple example, Newton's or Einstein's physics is not the same as that of Aspect, Clauser, and Zeilinger, just as modern psychology can't be compared to that of Wundt or Freud. Even medicine, though it has a solid foundation of scientific knowledge, is influenced by *probabilistic* factors, especially when it comes to complex diagnostic and therapeutic decisions, as well as by the environmental conditions in which a living being is placed. Yet, they all contributed to the knowledge we have today, and denying their *relative validity* would mean losing useful information that has led to certain results.

Therefore, confining everything that characterizes human existence, including the world of work, within a *box*, there's the risk of hindering the process of *awareness* necessary for the growth and development of our knowledge and our society. As previously mentioned, therefore, in the role of an *observer*, I will try to offer the reader my *interpretation* of these topics, fully aware that I will not provide them with any *universal* solution to their enigmas.

Indeed, each of us must take on the responsibility of finding the right path that will lead them to the answers they seek, avoiding delegating this task to others out of fear of failure or inability to face the difficulties they will encounter along the way.

It is likely that my attempt will end in *failure*, nonetheless it will have been a way to reflect once again on one of the most controversial and fundamental aspects of our social life: work.

Chapter 2

Awareness about Our Social Culture

Often, the price of *progress* is the renunciation of what truly had *value*. In the past two centuries, we have witnessed significant social development linked both to a new awareness of the individual about their own existence and to the development of science and technology applied to many aspects of our daily lives. However, this *evolution* has not always resulted in an improvement over the previous condition, but in many cases, in a standstill or even in a deterioration of the social status and the existential state of people.

These outcomes are often related to the interaction of two specific *factors*: whether the research and, consequently, the discoveries of the innovations were a result of human development, or, on the contrary, whether they influenced the habits and behaviors of individuals within their reality.

Indeed, the fundamental difference between these two paths lies in the fact that, in the first case, it is *humanity*, evolving through a series of experiences, that has *influenced* scientific, technological, and humanistic research and development to obtain *tools* that meet their new *condition*; in the second case, however, it was the *discovery* that induced a change to which individuals had to adapt, often quickly and with difficulty, exposing them to significant psychological and physical discomfort.

To give a simple and recent example, it is enough to recall the case of the telephone. A device created to bring people *closer* together and satisfy their need to communicate more quickly and over long distances, which today, represented by the *smartphone*, has become one of the main causes for creating the opposite effect, namely, distancing them from real life. Indeed, not only do people pay more attention to the screen of a smartphone than to the reality around them, but those who do not own this device and the services it offers risk being *marginalized* by both the primary and secondary groups to which they belong.

For this reason, its use lacks the *awareness* needed to protect individuals from unpleasant consequences, such as detachment from reality and direct contact with others, suffering from the release of *private* material or false information to the outside world without their consent, fraud attempts, etc. Yet, there are other examples like the telephone, such as atomic energy, the internet, electronic currencies, etc., which demonstrate how their conception preceded the necessary awareness to use them wisely.

As an integral part of society, work has also been subject to this type of *approach*: the first and perhaps most significant change with rapid and unpredictable effects, not only within this environment but also in the social context, can be represented by the *industrial revolutions*. Besides the great technological and scientific innovations, this event was characterized by its incisiveness because "*the faster its effects, the more prodigious the results that led to a revolutionary transformation in human life and perspectives[1]*" and not always with positive outcomes. The use of new machines, especially in the manufacturing sector, obviously brought the advantage of increasing various productions, but on the other hand, it reduced work to monotonous, repetitive, and exhausting sequences of movements that caused frequent injuries and, consequently, the interruption of the production.

Previously, and more precisely around the second half of the nineteenth century, thanks to the physiologist Wilhelm Wundt[2] and the Leipzig school, psychology was recognized as an experimental and autonomous science. Psychological phenomena began to be analyzed with experimental procedures, marking the

---

[1] Geoffrey Barraclough, *Guida alla storia contemporanea* - Ed. Laterza, 2004.
[2] *Wilhelm Wundt*. Trovato il 22 Luglio 2024 su *Enciclopedia Britannica*. Enciclopedia Britannica, Inc.

beginning of that journey that will lead, in the centuries to come, to all those discoveries and developments that would see this discipline explore every aspect of people's lives, including work.

With the new forms of work in the post-industrial revolution era, *Industrial and Organizational Psychology* was born, with the aim to analyze and try to solve concrete industry problems, particularly related to work organization and employee's selection. Hugo Münsterberg[3], a German psychologist and founder of *applied psychology*, laid the foundations of *Industrial psychology* by conducting studies on monotony, fatigue, adaptation to the work environment, and the first analyses of consumer motivation and sales techniques.

In that historic period the *scientific organization of work* was discussed to improve productivity, and the psychological component played only an ancillary role, more focused on avoiding the *accidents* to assembly lines and finding suitable profiles to hire for those specific tasks: the idea was to optimize the movements to be performed, along with those techniques related to the search and training of

---

[3] Hugo Münsterberg. Trovato il 22 Luglio 2024 su *Enciclopedia Britannica*. Enciclopedia Britannica, Inc.

employees who could carry out the job in the best and most efficient way possible.

The study that *scientifically* documented the link between social elements, such as group relationships and teamwork, with tangible elements like productivity and results, was conducted by Elton Mayo at the Hawthorne Works of Western Electric[4]: the aspect to consider in this case is not directly related to the variable connected to the employee's psychology, which gained a different value compared to the past, more prominent in relation to company production, but to the fact that Mayo and colleagues started this research to discover how workers' performance varied with changes in environmental conditions.

No one imagined they would take a different direction, more focused on the *emotional* involvement of individuals toward the company and the work they were assigned. Motivations, social needs, expectations, consideration, are just some of the points that scholars started to observe with respect to people's behavior in a working environment, to the

---

[4] Mayo, E. (1933). *The Human Problems of an Industrial Civilization.* New York: The Macmillan Company.

intensity of efforts applied to perform a specific job, and to their own physical and mental health.

It was thus by *chance* that researchers began to draw conclusions about the *individual-work* relationship in this sense: therefore, the hypothesis that much of the initial awareness by workers and managerial groups about their role within a company could depend on a kind of *social influence* determined by these discoveries is real and not to be ignore when we try to choose an interpretive key to understanding today's events.

Indeed, in a *system* where *certainty* of rules, working hours to meet, labor-wage compromise, but also the *coldness* of hierarchical power, unconditional consent, and competition at all levels, had always dominated, the *emotional* component of individuals has challenged, and continues to challenge today, the approach to work management that everyone was and is used to: these are indeed opposing concepts, hard to *align* within the same contextual core, unless through both a cultural and emotional development of the people involved.

The same researches conducted over the years have *almost* always supported this claim, as the results obtained have (almost) never been completely positive or negative, but rather partial and certainly *encouraging*. At the same time, however, they have added *new variables* to the productivity equation, such as motivations, needs, expectations, etc., which professionals could no longer ignore.

Applying these discoveries to reality, however, presupposed and still presupposes the need to *restructure* deep-seated aspects within, not only in corporate organizational cultures, but also into the social culture in which an individual develops: this is a hard task, considering that both included the *history*, *traditions*, and *symbols* that have represented for decades both social and work relationships and dynamics between individuals.

Therefore, the process of change that was intended to be implemented as a result of all those *unexpected* discoveries did not take into account the *experiential* journey that people would need to undertake to reach this level of awareness on multiple levels, not just on the professional one. Understanding does not come exclusively from *scientific rigor* but also from an *empirical* and *philosophical* aspect connected to the awareness of one's status and limits, both personal and operational, to evolve into something new and better: it is not possible to *humanize* work if we do not first make ourselves more *human*.

What has resulted is the perpetuation of that advocated process of *renovation* that can't be concluded precisely because of the lack of *awareness* required by people to implement it. On a *superficial* level, in the *image* that a company or a leader externally shows, it is indeed possible to highlight a different narrative from the past and that draws its energy from these new theories: nevertheless, it is almost impossible to find the same change at *deeper* levels, where individual awareness directly influences their behaviors, emotional responses, ethics, and morality.

This condition, as often appears, is not determined by the direct *responsibility* of companies, leaders, and employees involved in the modern working world, nor by the *ineffectiveness* of the strategies they have adopted to manage a working environment: what is missing is the *macro-change* that should occur at a cultural and social level to *develop* individuals with a different awareness of human existence and all those aspects with which they interact, including the world of work.

Thus, to conclude, the academic world that intervenes to study and, where possible, improves the work environment can't simply exclude from the obtained results the *motivations* related to their interventions, the *knowledge* and *intensity* they use to apply them, their own *cultural* and *academic* level: to understand what a *vase* represents, one must know the *potter* who created it. As we will see later, the *cultural* aspect, *psychology*, *knowledge*, and *awareness* of the people involved within an organization are fundamental in order to implement certain behaviors and management strategies.

Chapter 3

The Cultural Influence on Leadership Selection

Searching for something in a place where you know it doesn't exist is like chasing a dream within an illusion. Over the past few years, I have had the opportunity to attend several online webinars where trainers and coaches discussed their professional experiences and the techniques they employed within the companies where they were invited to train leaders.

One aspect that struck me in their testimonies, I also encountered in two training courses I attended – and which I will address further later on, was the recurring skepticism from many participants regarding the topics covered and the proposed strategies. During the webinars, I had the chance to interact with the consultants and ask them the same question, and that is if these *misunderstandings* were caused due to a lack of specific *personal* skills required for leadership, *essential* for fulfilling this type of role, rather than aspects related to their professional experience.

The answer I received from one of these consultants best represents what all of them tried to explain to me from their perspectives, which I report here: "*I hope that in the future, we will become much more aware of the kind of leadership traits and behaviors in relation to others, because we see people with the best professional performance being promoted as leaders, but this does not actually make them great leaders.*[5]"

Of course, one could *dismiss* these accounts as lacking in scientific *evidence* or, at most, in *statistical data* from other companies, since we are discussing about only four or five testimonies. However, a minimal awareness when analyzing the current situation is enough to realize that these are not isolated cases.

A recent example from the post-pandemic period, possibly linked to individuals' newfound awareness of their existence and, by extension, their roles within the workplace, is the unexpected wave of *voluntary resignations* that affected a significant portion of the workforce. In addition to this event, we could also mention the frequent failure to reach *fair* agreements that satisfy both employers and job seekers, as well as *statistics* on work-related stress, burnout, and turnover, which have long threatened employee health and the synergy and effectiveness of the work group itself.

---

[5] Session "Psychological Safety at Work" (https://www.linkedin.com/events/6986336540587126785/comments/ - min 45:11)".

The Leader and his own leadership should be the *tool* to balance and, where possible, improve these situations, regulate interpersonal interactions, and develop competencies, etc. However, it is crucial to assess whether leaders possess the necessary qualities to assume this role and carry it out successfully, especially at the time of their selection.

The consultant highlighted during the webinar three crucial, interconnected aspects of leadership: the *promotion/hiring* of certain profiles that possess and exhibit specific *traits/behaviors* aimed to achieve specific *outcomes*. Indeed, if the wrong profile is selected during the recruitment process, how can we expect that individual to develop high-quality leadership? And since these *traits* and *behaviors* are linked to human psychology, how can we expect a training course or webinar to improve, change, or even *create* such characteristics from scratch, when, as the existing scientific literature confirms, more complex *processes* are required, involving not only individuals' willingness to *change* but also the collaboration with specialists in psychology?

As previously mentioned, society's *culture* directly influences people's personalities and perceptions. This analysis helps explain the difficulties encountered by the trainers interviewed in the webinars. Without delving too deeply into details, the *theory of ecological systems*[6], later renamed the *bioecological model*[7] for its recognition of the relevance of biological and genetic aspects of individuals, highlights how various *systems* (five were hypothesized) influence an individual's life course: Urie Bronfenbrenner examines human development through the study of how humans create the specific environments in which they live. In other words, individuals develop according to their environmental context, which can include society as a whole and the era in which they live, both of which influence their behavior and development. In this view, *behavior* and *development* share a symbiotic relationship.

Going into details in the workplace, a simple example can illustrate my point of view: let's imagine we are in a room with a group of employees from the same department, with the same knowledge of tasks, the same work experience, and the same years of seniority. When asked, *"Who would like to assume a*

---

[6] Bronfenbrenner, U. (1979). *The Ecology of Human Development.* Cambridge, Massachusetts, and London, England: Harvard University Press

[7] Bronfenbrenner, U. (2004). *Making Human Beings Human.* Cornell University: Sage Publication

leadership role in our company?" what would their response be?

Contrary to what one might expect, not everyone would raise their hand to volunteer. A better salary and status are not needs that hold the same value for everyone. Some see career advancement as a natural goal in their professional journey, while others prefer to avoid this option due to the increased responsibilities, extended working hours, and conflicts to resolve, etc.

For those who would volunteer, one characteristic that is perceived as *essential* for taking on managerial roles today is *ambition*. Job advertisements frequently include this term among other requirements such as *talent*, *extensive work experience*, etc., which are often considered *necessary* credentials for aspiring to management positions. While the debate on this selection criterion is ongoing, it is interesting to explore the source of one's ambition.

Western cultures are typically considered *individualistic*, where people are encouraged to focus on themselves and pursue personal goals: there is a strong emphasis on personal ambition, success measured through one's career or financial gain, and continuous development. Actually, the control over one's destiny is believed to lie in individual choices that actively shape life's circumstances.

From an early age, individuals are *pushed* to prove they are better than others: parents, for example, tend to emphasize their children's *early* development, such as speaking or walking, or talents in sports or arts, etc. and comparing them to others. This *competition* becomes more pronounced in school and, ultimately, in the workplace, becoming an integral part of everyone's life.

Generosity and altruism towards others are often viewed as signs of weakness or personal failure, especially if it *helps* someone else succeed: this belief, that helping others leads to personal *fiasco*, undermines self-esteem and the group's respect which, in fact, fosters cooperation among individuals. Thus, in this part of the world, ambition is not seen as achieving *collective* success but rather *personal* success, and thus implies a natural disinterest in matters that do not directly concern oneself, regardless of the potential consequences or benefits that may arise.

However, as previously mentioned, new leadership theories emphasize the importance of *interpersonal* competencies as fundamental characteristics a leader should possess. These skills, referred to as *soft skills*, include problem-solving, empathy, effective communication, creativity, teamwork, and more. All these qualities aim to strengthen group dynamics at the expense of personal interests: studies over the years have shown that a leader is not only responsible for *task-related* duties but also for *relationships-interactions*, i.e., relating to employee interactions and support, which are essential for establishing a healthy and effective working environment.

The lack of the aforementioned qualities renders an individual incapable of exercising a certain type of leadership, or doing so without full *awareness*, focusing solely on the superficial aspects of their actions. This can lead to *cognitive dissonance* within the group being managed, causing members to experience discomfort and even conditions well-known to experts in the field.

Professionals in Human Resources may rightly argue that while *operational* competencies are easier to *assess* and more critical for assuming a specific role, *personal* qualities, often *claimed* by a candidate, are harder to verify: it is indeed undeniable that a job interview or an aptitude test, undeniably valid, are self-reported and insufficient to *uncover* such traits.

Nevertheless, regardless of any objections raised, it is indisputable that the selection strategies and the approach adopted in these contexts - by both the candidate and the selector - are closely linked to the culture in which they develop: it is indeed irrefutable that emphasis is placed on personal ambitions, seniority, work-related competencies, and even purely *social connections*, which may be unrelated to the skills required for high-level leadership but still crucial in the relational dynamics that naturally arise within an organization.

As explained by the consultants during the webinar, it later becomes the task of training courses and the strategies they promote to attempt to *cultivate* in leaders those qualities such as empathy, emotional intelligence, flexibility, creativity, critical thinking, proactivity, and others necessary to fulfill their role in the most effective and modern way possible. However, if the essential motivation and personal characteristics needed to fully understand the true value of these skills are missing, as well as the ability to apply them correctly, this training path will be *ineffective*.

Even considering the biology of individuals, particularly the *neuroplasticity* of the human brain and nervous system that is, the capacity to *change*, think differently, learn new things, modify behavior, and adapt quickly to new challenges, which is *active* in childhood and throughout development - this ability *declines* in adulthood. While not lost entirely, it can only be *reactivated* through considerable effort, triggering a series of neuromodulators related to alertness (epinephrine) and concentration (acetylcholine) to integrate new information into existing neural networks.

This exertion is difficult to achieve without motivational involvement, the pursuit of specific goals, or an intrinsic desire to modify one's personality. In the context of Western culture, an individual should relinquish *attachment* to a *self-centered status* within a hypothetical social or corporate hierarchy and instead see themselves as a *tool* for achieving shared objectives.

Specifically, regarding leaders and their development, it is not enough to attend a lecture, read a book, or memorize rules: the first step is recognizing *something* - a feeling, the need to learn, or the desire to improve - that activates the will to alter those neural pathways connected to previous cultural knowledge.

It is not, in fact, leadership style itself that creates the discomfort often observed within modern companies, but rather the discrepancy between the *image* projected outwardly and the *reality* experienced internally. For instance, having an organization or leader who claims to use strategies focused on considering the workgroup, empathetic leadership, active listening, and so forth, yet who in practice pursues the exact opposite, results in complex problems both at the organizational climate level and on a personal level.

For example, this happens when an individual moves from the satisfaction experienced upon being hired to a state of personal discomfort caused by the unmet promises of the initial job description. In the best-case scenario, this discrepancy is not too wide, and the employee adapts to the *emotional* standards of their colleagues, perhaps finding solace in the social support of the group or their private life to counterbalance the disappointment. In the worst-case scenario, however, this leads to psychological distress, prompting the individual to leave the *new* job or take an extended period of sick leave.

These are frequent occurrences, often justified by the saying *it's a job, not a hobby* or similar phrases, which imply that it is normal to experience negative feelings in a work environment. Yet, this is where most of one's time is spent, where relational skills are engaged at multiple levels, where economic resources for daily survival are obtained, and where one's mood and behavior are most affected.

Therefore, the change we should aspire to is not limited to this dimension alone but extends to the entire broader social and cultural system, influencing *lower-level* systems such as the workplace. The attempt to intervene on just this *subsystem*, as is happening now, tends to be obstructed by *cultural* barriers that limit the effectiveness of such efforts, limiting them to merely attach to its surface.

However, *acknowledging* the existence of these *obstacles* and their threat to the realization of modern management strategies does not prevent a company and its Human Resources department from aspiring to the changes theorized today. Referring to Bronfenbrenner's bioecological theory, although the Macrosystem directly influences the Microsystem, the latter can still *grow* independently of the former, with values and behaviors that are less *commonly* used in the broader context in which it is embedded.

Despite the predominance of *individualism* in today's society, certain dispositions - such as *respect*, *ethics*, and *transparency* - are still present and if they will apply within the communicative and interactional processes used by individuals and, of course, by companies themselves, can bypass the norms that hinder progress toward something better and achievable, as demonstrated by studies conducted thus far.

When these elements are deeply embedded in organizational cultures, the ideal conditions will emerge, allowing certain social constructs to lose their influence over the actions and decisions made in this regard: instead, the focus will shift directly to the interactions and behaviors exhibited by individuals within these cultures and to the selection of candidates for the future, ensuring a workforce in tune with modern times.

Although a jar of sweets may contain various shapes and flavors, with less sugar or made with vegetable gelatin, a person with diabetes will still suffer from a stomach ache, albeit of varying intensity: although the positive and negative aspects of modern leaders are continually assessed, the *pool* and *methodologies* used for their selection are invariably tied to those of a past that, at least in the academic world, one would prefer to move beyond.

Changing these selection criteria should be a priority for companies to more easily implement the most modern management techniques.

Chapter 4

Leader Development and Leadership: An Individual Commitment to Achieving a Collective Goal

Self-development is the primary mission of every individual, as only through personal growth we can contribute to building a better world. As previously mentioned, with the emergence of new forms of work following the industrial revolution and the advent of Industrial and Organizational Psychology, both companies and scholars began focusing on the design of specific *training* programs: these programs should enable workers to quickly and effectively learn the movements necessary for performing their job tasks. At the same time, managers are being *trained* to select and manage the new workforce in order to achieve corporate goals.

Anyway, *training* is no longer understood as the mere transfer of *knowledge* from father to son to maintain a family business or work the fields upon reaching adulthood: instead, it is entrusted to experts who *plan* its implementation and target groups of individuals who need to become *specialists* in their assigned tasks. However, when discussing training today, it is no longer possible to focus solely on the development of *professional skills*, which pertain to the most practical aspects, such as *manual* and *procedural knowledge* related to specific tasks: indeed, such training can also involve *relational skills*, which are crucial in managing work teams and ensuring the success of organizations. Clearly, while the first type of training has tangible *outcomes* in the performance of tasks - such as demonstrating the ability to assemble or operate machinery, knowing and applying regulations, responding to customer inquiries, etc. - in the second case, it may not always be as *evident* or *manifest* as in the first.

Some years ago, I had the opportunity to attend two courses on basic personnel management techniques, organized by two distinct entities: the first was offered within a university setting and led by a trainer with previous leadership experience. The second was organized by the company I worked for and carried on by an occupational psychologist.

Participants in the first course held responsibility roles within their respective companies, which operated in different sectors of production and services. The second course was attended by colleagues with managerial and supervisory roles. Both courses covered topics related to processes aimed at involving employees in leadership development, the use of communication as a management tool, the application of situational leadership, and conflict and interview management. Since these strategies inherently require the use of specific *relational* skills, both courses also included a section dedicated to exploring theories of individual psychology. This allowed participants not only to explore different personality types that may be present in a work group but also to examine their own personality type.

One interesting observation, which I later encountered in conversations with other participants in similar courses, relates to the feedback shared by participants at the end of both training programs - particularly in the university-based course, where the group was more *diversified* in terms of professional profiles and less directly influenced by company expectations. Many of them, indeed, claimed that they had more doubts than when they began the course, and they were unsure how to apply what they had learned to their organizational contexts.

To better understand the challenges faced by these participants, we can refer to the statements made by experts in the previously mentioned webinars: specific personal qualities are required to *deliver* a leadership style that maximizes results and fosters the well-being of the work group. Translating this concept to training, the same *mindset* is essential to appropriately *understand* the information received from external sources, including that coming from a training process.

Encouraging an individual to embark on such a journey to acquire or improve specific *personal skills* without genuine *commitment* on their part, risks *undermining* its effectiveness. Additionally, it may create *misunderstandings* with the company and the work group: often, this individual already holds a *leadership role*, perhaps with many years of experience, and may *perceive* this type of training as *criticism* of their work, which they had believed to be correct. Furthermore, as previously mentioned, the *desire* to develop in this area must be present: without strong and genuine motivation, it will be challenging to *engage* with deeper aspects of one's own personality.

Despite this, it is not possible to put all the responsibility onto a leader or a company's recruitment technique, which, as mentioned by experts in the webinar, often reveal *technical gaps* in identifying candidates or employees with the *psychological traits* necessary for certain roles: as numerous studies demonstrate, given certain motivational prerequisites, these traits can be developed and trained in individuals. Therefore, part of the problem should also be sought within the training process itself.

Indeed, training processes in general, including those in educational settings, often lack an *eclectic* vision and the *sharing* of knowledge that aims at *evolution* rather than *indoctrination* of people: the tendency is often to *impose*, and in some cases, *sell* knowledge not for its real *utility*, but because the level of *awareness* of those responsible for teaching has not allowed them to *comprehend* anything beyond it.

Reflecting on the courses I attended, a second aspect that connects to this is precisely the content and the interpretations accompanying each topic discussed: although the trainers came from two different professional backgrounds - one more *practical* and the other more *academic*, intrinsic to the psychology of the individual - both *explored* the same theories that, over the years, have influenced modern psychology and found significant applications in the workplace in the attempt to understand and guide behaviors within it.

Maslow's hierarchy of needs[8], Hersey and Blanchard's situational leadership[9] and also concepts such as archetypes like the Prima Donna or Pragmatist[10] are just a few of the theories used in both courses, on which the proposed exercises were based. Clearly, the validity of these theories is unquestionable, yet it raises the question of whether the *context* in which they were presented was flawed.

To explain this idea more clearly, it is essential to consider that participants are generally individuals who have long since left the school or university environment, or who may never have pursued such paths, coming to their current job roles solely due to the professional skills acquired through years of work experience. Placing them again, years later or for the first time, in front of a *desk* with a considerable and often unnecessary amount of *data* to study risks turning them into those elementary school children who had to learn a poem by heart: after many readings and through repetition, they might even be

---

[8] Maslow, A. H. (1943). A theory of human motivation. *Psychological Review*. 50(4), 370–396.
[9] Hersey, P. Blanchard, K. (1969). *Management of Organizational Behavior: Utilizing Human Resources*. Englewood Cliffs, New Jersey: Prentice Hall.
[10] Hein, H. (2009) *Motivation: Motivationsteori og praktisk anvendelse*. Copenhagen: Hans Reitzels Forlag.

able to remember every strophe, but few would understand its structure and real meaning.

To apply *theory* to *practice*, especially in this field, a different kind of *process* is required—one that goes beyond mere *memorization* of concepts: companies and their employees do not need leaders capable of listing the basic principles of *effective leadership*, explaining the *four theoretical paradigms* on which these processes are based, or explain a leadership style at a staff meeting that they will never be able to implement in practice.

Unfortunately, modern training often relies on a predominantly *educational* and not *experiential* teaching methodology. Bringing leaders in a classroom to explain various theories of modern psychology or engaging them in group activities like dancing and solving quizzes to foster teamwork and collaboration is not the most effective way to address complex corporate challenges.

On television, we often see films where a wealthy individual chooses to spend some time in a ghetto to understand what it means to be poor. However, throughout this experience, the protagonist knows that sooner or later, they will return to their privileged life, and that the reality they are living in that moment is not, and never will be, their own. With this mindset, it is impossible to truly grasp what it means to face problems like securing food for oneself and one's family, being unable to pay bills or rent, or struggling to find a job. Only by forgetting what they had, they could fully understand that experience from the right perspective.

The same applies in the workplace, especially when addressing the principles of training and leadership: how many people can truly say they have abandoned the egocentrism that is *naturally* acquired from the society in which they develop, to embark on an experiential journey that first changes their perception of what they already know and of the people they work with? How many, for instance, can claim to have personally experienced or to have truly *empathized* through the experiences of others, a toxic work environment with no alternative but to endure it until they are utterly exhausted? Or to have experienced burnout, depression, stress, and other challenges in a way that allows them to fully understand the meaning of these terms?

Often, the outcome of leadership and training is directly correlated with the experiential journey of the individuals who deliver them: if their understanding of certain concepts is only *superficial*, then the impact of their interventions will be equally limited, focusing solely on the *image* they project outward, but irrelevant to the reality in which they are integrated.

The greatest challenge we face today is learning to recognize our own limitations: unfortunately, the Western world, as mentioned earlier, is characterized by egocentrism, which, even in training, leads to prioritizing personal knowledge and interests over those of others.

All training, including school systems, is influenced by this culture: knowledge is *imposed* rather than *shared* between teachers and students. Teachers should be able to *show* the students their knowledge without imposing it, *adapting* it to the context in which they operate: at the same time, students should be *willing* to engage in this learning process to understand, without being coerced, the *knowledge* made available to them.

Paulo Freire, a renowned Brazilian educator and philosopher, defined training as follows: "*the one who teaches learns by teaching, and the one who learns teaches by learning, as we are continuously forming ourselves*"[11]. Today, people are often *anchored* to the knowledge they have managed to understand, considering *superfluous*

---

[11] Freire, P. (2004). *Pedagogia dell'autonomia. Saperi necessari per la pratica educativa*. Torino: EGA.

everything their *awareness* has not allowed them to grasp.

Yet, a leader who attends a training course is typically seeking *practical* solutions to apply to their working environment, rather than a re-examination of major theories in psychology or leadership paradigms. An approach which is *abstract* and *disconnected* from the context in which they are actively engaged is likely to demotivate them and fail to trigger that emotional and intellectual involvement necessary to activate the neurological components previously mentioned, that lead to the actual development required.

Trainers should first and foremost *understand* the individuals they are training and adapt their teaching style to their personalities and working realities, not the other way around. They should delve deeply into the world of the trainees, the key players within it, and explore the issues that hinder the realization of certain types of leadership, rather than offering a sterile explanation of abstract theory. If you don't understand the composition of the soil on which a certain type of seed is to be planted, the risk is that the entire crop will be compromised.

This process can be seen as an exchange of information between a trainer and their knowledge, and a leader or HR manager and their specific work situation: personalities and interactions among individuals cannot be placed into a one-size-fits-all box or classified according to a standard method that meets every type of need.

As previously mentioned, the knowledge of trainers, coaches, and business consultants is not being questioned; rather, it is the fact that this knowledge is often not *linked* to the training context in which they operate, nor to the *real-world* scenarios where the participants in their courses will apply it. It would be like using quantum physics to explain how to turn on a stove to cook an egg in a beginner's cooking class: though, theoretically, there might be a formula to explain every action performed by an expert chef, it would not be the most appropriate explanation for an audience that likely lacks the foundational knowledge or interest to fully understand it.

The world of modern training should reclaim this kind of *exploration* of the "other" in order to better direct subsequent interventions and achieve effective solutions. *Forcing* the use of a certain type of knowledge in the wrong context risks undermining its validity, as failure can lead to the perception of *ineffectiveness* due to the inability to produce the desired outcome.

The understanding of a *theory*, the development of a *method*, or the application of a *strategy* is directly linked to the knowledge and experience of those who devised them, the personalities of the participants, the relational dynamics, and the tasks in which these elements have been tested and later applied: what may seem valid in some circumstances may not be in others, even if similar, precisely because of these *imperceptible* variables. For instance, the *effect of the experimenter's expectations* is often significantly related to the outcome at the end of an observation: a manager might *loosen* control over employees to appear more benevolent and friendly to those evaluating them, including the company, or an employee may experience a boost in personal motivation to prove themselves capable of meeting the tasks assigned by researchers. These are *variables* that can influence the results of a study or the implementation of certain strategies in specific contexts to varying degrees.

However, just as it is not feasible to ask trainers to explore every single aspect of the lives of the scholars they reference or of the participants in the experiments they organize to fully understand the theories they draw upon, it is also unreasonable to expect these theories to be *universally* applicable to every context due to the lack of these critically important *details*. It seems that the world of training is *trapped* in what psychology defines as *heuristics*, or *mental shortcuts*, which characterize the cognitive processes of people in general. These are the unconscious rules used to reframe problems and transform them into simpler, almost automatic operations, thereby achieving more accessible and quicker solutions, which in turn produce judgments, formulate inferences and analogies, give meaning to certain experiences, and make decisions for complex problems or situational information.

Thanks to heuristics, individuals don't need to engage in deep reasoning every time they process data from the external world. However, precisely for this reason, heuristics can lead to errors in both judgment and decision-making. For example, when seeing a Lamborghini Diablo speeding down the road, it's easy to assume that the driver is wealthy and that the car is among the most powerful out there: alternative possibilities are not considered—such as the driver is not rich but rather renting the car to satisfy a whim—or reflecting on the remarkable development the automotive industry has undergone from the first steam-powered vehicle to that model.

In every aspect of life - from major existential issues, politics, and society to the realms of work and education - people's way of observing, analyzing, and behaving remains faithful to this heuristic system. This often results in neglecting many details in favor of swift conclusions that may prove vulnerable to errors in situations requiring a deeper and more logical analysis.

As a result, *reality* is often observed *unconsciously*, with individuals *passively* accepting what happens and accepting events as they appear and as *common sense* interprets them: yet, the difference lies precisely in acting *consciously*, *activating* the most appropriate strategies to analyze and interpret such events, thereby better guiding subsequent interventions. While it is *understandable* to expect the former approach from the *everyday* person, on the other hand those who *train* should, be more *aware*, open to *doubt* and *dialogue*, based on the premise that it is their knowledge what is made available to others, not the other way around: as Freire previously stated, the role of a trainer is not only to teach but also to *learn* from others through the understanding of those who come into the classroom seeking *information* that will serve their purposes, rather than generating further confusion. In this way, the *unidirectionality* of the training process ceases, and the *bidirectional* exchange and sharing of knowledge are activated.

As mentioned earlier, within the workplace microsystem, it is essential to intervene immediately to initiate a change that encourages companies to strengthen their selection processes and hire employees with appropriate personal and motivational skills, which form the foundation for developing future leaders: subsequently, companies should design a training process that meets their employees' needs and, combined with professional experience, prepares them to face their respective tasks in the most appropriate way.

This last part, however, is the responsibility of the trainers and depends on their approach with which they perform their duties - which should be more focused on the *individuals* being trained rather than on the *instructional* program itself. Therefore, a company can't simply *plan* a development strategy, especially if aimed at improving specific skills and applying certain strategies, without *unhooking* from the recruitment methods of the past, particularly concerning its leaders: the *search* should focus on the personalities and talents of individuals who can carry forward the company's *mission*, rather than those based solely on superficial *friendship* or *professional experience* gained over a medium-to-long period.

At the same time, trainers cannot rely on a hypothetical *manual* to be applied universally to every problem, as it should be clear so far that it's impossible to enclose all variables of a working environment withing a single box.

Chapter 5
Employees: An Active Part in Leadership Dynamics

The responsibilities of a group are the reflection of the leader's abilities, but it is the unity of the group that transforms visions into reality. In the early 1970s, psychologist Henri Tajfel and colleagues conducted the famous *Klee-Kandinsky experiment*[12] on *social judgment* theory: this experiment aimed to explore the internal processes of an individual's judgment, how easily people formed into groups, and the extent to which they tended to favor the in-group and discriminate against the out-group.

This paradigm underlies what is known as *social identity theory*[13], namely, those processes of categorization, identification, and social comparison that enable an individual to construct a *social self* and feel part of a specific group, consequently eliciting cognitive bias

---

[12] Tajfel, H., Flament. C., Billig, M. G. & Bundy, R. P. (1971). Social categorization and intergroup behaviour. *European Journal of Social Psychology*, *1*, 149-178.

[13] Tajfel, H. & Turner, J.C. (1979). *An integrative theory of intergroup conflict*. In W. G. Austin & S. Worchel (Eds), *The social psychology of intergroup relations*. (pp. 33-47). Monterey, CA: Brooks Cole.

mechanisms and favoritism behavior towards its members. However, an individual can simultaneously belong to different social groups, from family and friends to sports and cultural activities, as well as, of course, work-related groups: this belonging is linked to the sharing of the same values, ideas, and attitudes among members, which will determine that process of self-categorization to which the individual will refer every time they activate those comparative cognitive processes of stimuli coming from both the external and internal environment.

Yet, as Mowday and Sutton also assert, it is incorrect to depict members of a group, especially within an organization as cognitively *stylized* figures whose behavior is not influenced by emotions or interactions: categorization, in fact, also depends on their pre-existing set of expectations, goals, and theories that largely derive from their membership and their encounters within that group[14].

What happens, then, when the reference points that led to the aforementioned affiliation with that group change, or when it turns out that these reference points are entirely absent in a new group, despite the

---

[14] Mowday, R.T., Sutton, R.I. (1993). Organizational behaviour: linking individuals and groups to organizational context. *Annual Review of Psychology*, 44, 195-229.

initial assumptions? It often occurs within organizations that agreements presented prior to hiring are not subsequently respected, or an employer branding promises an organizational culture that is actually not present or still needs to develop in that specific company.

In some cases, it may occur that an individual activates that process of *depersonalization* mentioned by John Turner, which is the *self-stereotyping* through which the self ends up being perceived as interchangeable in a categorical sense with other group members. However, when these differences exceed those on which people's core constructs are based - such as those related to moral and ethical values, respect, and friendship, an individual may decide to leave that group or even oppose its members. In many cases, when the aforementioned strategies cannot be applied, the risk is to fall into states of depression or anxiety that undermine the health of individuals[15].

In discussions concerning *work*, experts frequently focus on the theme of leadership, including the professional and personal characteristics of a leader,

---

[15] Turner, J.C., Hogg, M.A., Oakes, P.J., Reicher, S.D., Wetherell, M.S. (1987). *Rediscovering the social group: A self-categorization theory*. Cambridge, MA, US: Basil Blackwell.

the strategies adopted to motivate, support, and develop employees' skills, as well as the resolution of issues and conflicts that may arise during their duties. Despite the extensive exploration of this subject, it is essential to recognize that employees and work groups play an intrinsic active role in these dynamics.

The literature about leadership describes theories that rightly consider the maturity, experience, and competence levels of employees as fundamental variables in determining which strategies should be adopted in a given context. For instance, according to Hersey and Blanchard's *situational leadership* theory[9], a leader's behavior must adapt according to the type of group: the maturity of collaborators serves as the essential point to establish leadership, intended as both professional experience and psychological development.

Regardless of the value that experts may assign to these schools of thought, it is undeniable that the personalities of employees cannot be overlooked when referring to their management and contributions to the organization, nor how they *categorize* themselves within the company and other contexts: they are not *passive* entities subjected to leadership; rather, their *actions*, even those of *non-*

intervention, will influence work dynamics and their own well-being.

To illustrate this concept of *passivity/reactivity*, reference can be made to toxic work environments where mobbing incidents, favoritism towards certain colleagues at the expense of others, lack of collaboration, and other behaviors deemed *ethically inappropriate* frequently occur: regardless of the underlying reasons for such situations, the passivity exhibited by employees in *enduring* or merely *observing* these actions absurdly represents a form of *consent*, accepting and supporting them. Similarly, in an environment characterized by oppositional traits, when an employee or a small group of colleagues introduces toxic *behaviors* that are likely to destabilize the established equilibrium, the response of others - including management - whether *tolerant* or *interventionist*, will ultimately determine the future of that working team.

From this consideration, two important conclusions can be drawn when analyzing a work environment and the implemented leadership style. The first is obviously related to the *expectations* regarding a leader's performance: as previously mentioned, a common error is to use a *one-sided* approach, overlooking the fundamental variables necessary in order to understand why certain strategies or interventions fail.

The success or failure of a team does not solely depend on who manages it but also on those who belong to it. The interactions occurring among individuals constitute a continuous exchange of *inputs* and *feedback* that shape their subsequent actions to achieve specific personal or group outcomes: thus, all individuals are active participants in the organizational life, even when this entails enduring toxic management or undermining stability through inadequate behaviors.

To articulate this in different terms, it's like balancing a glass on the edge of a table: *waiting* for it to fall or *pushing* it will result in the same *outcome* - having a broken glass. Using the *excuse* that, in the first case, the probability of it not falling was equal to the probability of it falling, or that it's not the direct *responsibility* of the observer to save the glass, is not sufficient to justify a behavior that would, in fact, would prevent having glass shards scattered across the floor: a hazardous *consequence* that could harm anyone, including the observer themselves. This example leads to the second important point to mention: just as a leader can influence the success or failure of a leadership style, the work group also has the *power* to *accept* or *oppose* the style employed for its management, as long as it acts as a cohesive rather than a separate entity.

This concept is rarely applied within the modern Western social context, characterized by the aforementioned individualistic culture. Indeed, in many cases, an employee may disregard the *situation* of a colleague being discriminated for fear of finding themselves in the so-called *eye of the storm*, or because they perceive such *violent* treatment as a justified consequence for that individual's *performance*, or even because they do not perceive their *role* or *personality* as capable of facing that situation.

Whatever the reason, the potential outcome that may arise in these situations, which remains *latent* beneath the surface of individuals' unconscious minds, is that such behaviors can affect everyone at any moment within organizational life, and they can lead individuals to experience an increase in personal dissatisfaction and may result in the possible collapse of the coping strategies implemented to counteract them, thereby posing the risk of developing pathologies related to such situations. Ultimately, the prospect of an employee with this experiential background assuming a managerial position.

All individuals should consider themselves *active* participants in the pursuit of their own dimension, well-being, and role, *collectively* contributing to the achievement of both personal and shared success according to the expectations and capabilities that each individual possesses and can offer to others: gaining this awareness not only expands the analytical framework regarding a work environment but also emphasizes that, thinking about the example of the broken glass, each individual is equally responsible for their actions and passivity, *shaping* the reality in which they are embedded, even the most complicated ones.

This analysis further highlights that not only do organizations and management bear *direct* responsibility for group management and working conditions, but employees themselves can also influence this aspect through their actions, regardless of their nature.

Thus, the cultural *limitations* previously mentioned hinder a *natural* adoption of a singular *worldview* that encompasses behaviors aimed at promoting the well-being of *both* individuals and organizations: simply claiming to have *acquired* these values because they have been imposed makes this action *artificial* and *ineffective*. These limitations can only be transcended through *social* change, for the benefit of all rather than just of a select number of individuals or organizational units.

In conclusion, in his poem "Invictus" William Ernest Henley states: "I am the master of my fate, I am the captain of my soul / I am the master of my fate, I am the captain of my soul". The work group, even if set in a toxic context, as previously mentioned, remains *aware* of what occurs around it and possesses the *knowledge* to respond accordingly: indeed, while it can support a particular management approach because it has the requisite *understanding* to recognize it is acting in the right direction, it can also oppose that same approach for the same reasons, but only as a united and cohesive entity.

Chapter 6

The Perception of Surrounding Reality: Deception or Lack of Information?

The reality around us is often deceptive, an incomplete canvas painted by our lack of information and biases. What has been written so far aims to demonstrate the *coexistence* of two opposing types of *culture* within organizations: the *individualistic* one, anchored in the dominant traits of Western society, where personal needs come before collective ones, hierarchies matter more than people, and meritocracy is secondary to favoritism, but most notably, where work life and private life are not balanced; on the other hand, the *knowledge-based* culture, which seeks to indicate the right direction to follow, drawing on studies conducted by experts, which are in a position diametrically opposed to the first.

The contrast between these two poles leads to a deadlock, where many of the concepts related to improving the working world fail to take root *deeply* in the *essence* of the key players involved - understood as companies, their leaders, and the employees themselves - but only remain at a *superficial* level, in the image they project externally. This aspect makes it difficult to understand what has truly been internalized and what is merely being used to conform to a strategically controversial *political correctness*.

The *subtle* difference between *appearance* and *reality* is perhaps more damaging than an *openly* negative situation, because in the first case, it becomes difficult to plan and implement *strategies* to solve a specific problem. Indeed, *efforts* to adopt behaviors deemed *correct* by *general opinion* in order to achieve an organizational goal, secure a promotion, or even avoid addressing crucial issues that could undermine certain power positions, are not *natural* but rather artificial and temporary: as a matter of fact, when the situation requires a prolonged effort and *deeper* commitment, the sacrifice needed to maintain this *mental state* overwhelms the individual's available *psychological energy*, and the *house of cards* collapses under the weight of responsibilities they should bear.

This phenomenon is characteristic of the development that society has undergone in recent decades regarding socially *critical* issues, and it is not limited to the working world, which reflects this system. For example, consider what is today called *subtle discrimination*: it is a sneaky, more hidden, and less obvious form of discrimination. Unlike more explicit or manifest forms that involve clearly discriminatory behaviors, subtle discrimination is often difficult to prove and risks rendering every form of counteraction ineffective.

Covert stereotypes, structural discrimination in hiring processes, microaggressions such as comments, actions, or attitudes that, even if seemingly harmless or accidental, can be offensive or harmful to people from certain groups, disparities in access to opportunities, implicit privileges: being more difficult to identify and address than open forms of discrimination, they have significant effects on the daily lives and opportunities of those affected. Addressing this issue requires critical awareness, a review of policies and practices, and a collective commitment to promote equality and justice.

Within organizations, the consequences of the coexistence of these two types of culture are evident and vary in their impact on people's lives: one example could be related to leaders who believe they have the personal skills to deliver a certain type of leadership but, when called upon to resolve specific situations or adopt targeted and appropriate behaviors to handle a given situation, they inevitably fail.

Another example mentioned previously refers to employees who, after feeling initial satisfaction from a new hire, perhaps following a long selection process, gradually experience personal discomfort: the involvement, commitment, and collaboration that the *new hire* initially exhibited begin to slowly disappear when the work reality or previously established agreements are not upheld.

This effect can be observed not only in the *field*, that is, in the daily actions of the individuals involved within organizations, but also within the *narrative* intrinsic into the messages, slogans, information, and the interpretation of certain *technicalities*, which *reflect* this cultural *dualism*. Its inappropriate use, framed within the workplace *ad proprium usum et consummationem* (for one's own use and benefit), instead of improving the organizational culture and climate, has the opposite, and perhaps more damaging, effect.

A current example in this regard is the recent juxtaposition by companies and human resources between the terms *family* and *workplace*: the intention is to convey the idea that a person will find in the workplace the same support, respect, and recognition that they assume to have in the family context. However, this form of comparison poses risks, especially the activation of controversial behaviors in individuals, often excessively reverent and sacrificial, which someone might exploit to their own advantage. Moreover, it may imply an expectation of *endless* dialogue and the sharing of *personal* matters with managers and colleagues, with the fear of being marginalized if one does not participate.

Although what has just been mentioned may suffice to reconsider this comparative approach, the concept of *family* in this context lacks all the other *nuances* that characterize the original one: in fact, a family unit is also marked by internal controversies, frictions, more or less serious discussions, acts of violence, separations, disrespect, and mistreatment. Thus, despite the fact that work and family spheres should always be kept separate for essentially *semantic* reasons and individual *balance*, the use of this juxtaposition is nonetheless *erroneous* and *misleading*, as it overlooks the real dynamics that, de facto, coexist within both dimensions. From this perspective, instead of appealing to *family values*, organizations should aim to foster values of mutual *respect*, *work ethics*, *dialogue*, and a rediscovery of those *principles* that should be the basis for all interactions and decisions affecting the workgroup.

Another term that is often *mishandled* by those in the field is *recognition*. There is an almost obsessive need to always and inevitably acknowledge *something* to others, especially to the employees, even the most insignificant detail, to boost their motivation and make them feel like an *integral* part of the company. Yet, *rare* things are also the most precious and valuable, and often, constantly giving *pats on the back* and saying *well done* for every task done *well* diminishes the true significance of those words.

It seems as if there is a lack of awareness that employees come from a specific experiential and educational background, sometimes even better than that of a manager or human resources worker, so that they develop precise inferences about the reality around them and do not always *passively* accept leadership as they did in past centuries.

During one of the annual reviews aimed at assessing my job competencies and finding ways to further develop them, my manager opened with this *textbook-perfect leader* phrase: "*You are an important asset to the company and are doing an excellent job.*" Regardless of the fact that my tasks were a series of routine actions, a *cog* in a bigger machine that could have been *rewarded* in other ways, the last time he had shown any interest in me or my contribution was exactly one year earlier, during the same review: no interaction, no meetings, not even an informal conversation had taken place in the time between the two events. So, how could he claim what he was saying if, during all this time, he had not had any direct contact with me or regular feedback on my performance?

Moreover, given the nature of my work and my experience, the *room* for improvement was limited and could at most suggest a promotion: unfortunately, within that organizational culture, not only was there no clear and specific advancement plan to reference, but there was also no willingness, especially from the management team, to walk that path with me. These conditions rendered that questionnaire ineffective and, more importantly, emptied the manager's words of *recognition* of any real meaning.

These inferences are made by anyone and serve to authenticate the behavior of others: if this latter is not consistent with the message accompanying it, the resulting dissonance can produce opposite responses to those aimed by that the *textbook* recognition.

The same applies to the use of these *questionnaires* to measure any characteristic of the employee, such as their skills or performance, that is of interest to the company: too often, they are conducted inconsistently and without continuous interaction between employees and managers. Returning to my previous experience, interest in a person's development should be seen as a task to be carried out periodically throughout the year, not on rare occasions.

Moreover, as happens in many organizational settings, the results of these tests are often an end in themselves, especially when it comes to career advancement or a new hire: even if they confirm that an employee meets the requirements for a certain role, or that a candidate is better qualified than another, in the end, it will always be those previously mentioned internal dynamics,, to determine who gets the position.

Regarding this last point, the slogans connected to it, such as *"By promoting or hiring the wrong people, we start losing the best ones"*, appear as *self-contradictory paradoxes* that affirm and deny their meaning simultaneously, as they are hard to prove: indeed, going back to what was said previously about the behavior directly connected to social and cultural norms, even a recruiter is influenced by these factors when having to choose between an individual with whom they share certain characteristics, not necessarily *professional*, and another who is simply qualified for the job; or when receiving a *recommendation* from a superior or colleague regarding someone they believe should hold a certain position. Is it really possible to determine or admit that the wrong person was *hired* or *promoted*?

These *contradictions* also affect the *technicalities* that should be *objective* but are instead subject to the most convenient interpretation assignable. In this regard, there has recently been a lot of *focus* on contrasting two leadership styles identified as *Boss* and *Leader*, often used to describe a manager's behavior with a negative connotation in the first case, and a positive one in the second.

For example, messages like these are often conveyed: *"The Boss directs and commands"* vs. *"The Leader consults and delegates"*; *"The Boss controls"* vs. *"The Leader inspires"*; *"The Boss doesn't allow others to express themselves and grow"* vs. *"The Leader listens and shape"*.

These are just a few of the several comparisons used by many experts, particularly in human resources, to put in contrast those who exhibit *appropriate* behavior in managing a team and those who do not: yet, as just mentioned, these are two very distinct leadership styles, and when placed within specific work contexts, the *positive-negative* connotation they try to convey loses its meaning.

In fact, the *Boss* as described in the literature refers to a leadership style more focused on *tasks* than *relationships* and is *properly* applicable in many work environments such as a metalworking or metallurgical industry, where the tasks performed, as well as the interactions between employees and the management group, limit the management options available to a leader.

It is the context, shaped by the *dynamics* that develop between the company, the tasks to be performed, and the work group, that determines which type of management is most suitable to apply. A leader's actions are not *static* but rather a dynamic *adaptation* to regulate the interactions between these three elements: they perform a sort of *homeostatic* function when an event destabilizes their balance.

Let's think about working at a blast furnace or on an assembly line: the margin for *delegation* and *consultation* by a leader in their interactions with a worker is not as wide as it might be within a team that designs airplanes or cars. Similarly, *inspiring* and *motivating* an employee who spends all day performing standard movements at a machine to assemble parts is not as easy as, for example, with someone working in a marketing office: of course, even in the former case, there are motivational systems focused on *rewards*, which might be represented by production bonuses, salary increases, reduced working hours, etc., and on a more *relational* level, by openness to dialogue, emotional support, and mutual respect.

On the contrary, the more *dynamic* a context is - meaning more tasks to perform, more interactions to deal with between colleagues, and more projects to follow - the more choices a manager will have and need to make. Thus, a *Boss* placed in such a work environment could be counterproductive, while a *Leader* in the opposite context may be ineffective.

Therefore, it is *misleading* to use the peculiar traits of a leadership style to *label* a leader as incapable of doing their job: there are no good or bad leadership, but rather leaders with or without the *professional* and *personal qualities* that enable them to act appropriately in a specific work context.

Another slogan that opens up for consideration is: *A leader does not create followers but other leaders*". In this case, it would also be necessary to specify which context this statement should refer to - whether within a corporate environment or limited to the educational sphere. In fact, the possibility that a manager at the height of their career would choose to hire employees with better abilities than their own and be willing to *develop* them in this regard - risking, as often happens, being *replaced* by their own *protégé* - is very unlikely today and limited to specific contexts.

There are certainly companies that can boast well-defined and well-studied advancement and training plans designed to respect and protect their leaders and employees. Nevertheless, there are many cases where a manager above forty has found themselves, without a job and perhaps with a family to support: these situations happen frequently, especially to those who failed to *reinvent* themselves and to keep *pace* with progress, ending up in a spiral characterized by long periods of unemployment, alternated with part-time, lower-paying jobs than a management position, without protections for injuries or illness. From this perspective, many leaders prefer to maintain a position of *advantage* over their workgroup and even their closest collaborators.

Also from a *work system* perspective, it is evident how many *innovations* continue to face strong resistance from old habits. This is the case, for example, with Smart Working. In fact, this system was intended to bring not only the balance between private life and work that had been discussed earlier, but also *significant* advantages in terms of production. Yet, its widespread use had to wait for a *tragic* period of general lockdown to occur to make many companies realize that the logic of *controlling* employees through a *physical workspace* was flawed and, in some cases, counterproductive, if replaced by a focus on *goals* to be achieved and the *management* of their own working times.

Later, in further confirmation that the issue is not *technical* but *cultural*, after the pandemic, new types of *conflicts* arose between companies and employees - characterized by those who wanted to return to *old* habits and those who wished to continue in that direction or, at most, embrace *hybrid* alternatives. Regardless of the specific reasons behind this kind of *dispute*, two fundamental aspects that characterized the relationship between employers and employees during this period went unnoticed: firstly, the full *collaboration* and *trust* that was established despite the distance; secondly, closely related to the first, the opportunity to embrace an *ethic* of work that sees all parties directly and mutually responsible for their well-being and their economy.

The fundamental aspects that unite these examples, and all others that could be made, are essentially the same ones from which all the discomfort people experience in the workplace generates and the foundation from which analysis and action should begin: change does not come simply from applying modern theories to the world of work; rather it comes from the awareness of the cultural limitations that shape the beliefs and values resisting those *improvements* which are being asked to be implemented.

Experts in this field are aware that certain strategies and behaviors are necessary to improve the organizational climate and culture, in order to keep companies competitive over time: however, this *awareness* alone is not enough to embed certain types of interventions deeply if those involved lack specific personal qualities.

In fact, there is no deliberate *intent* by individuals to act wrongly or inappropriately within the work dynamics where their skills are engaged: on the contrary, it is simply the natural activation of certain behaviors linked to those human constructs that characterize this society, making that particular response seem *logical*. Scientific *discovery* or an emotionally significant *event* does not have the *power* to trigger a *complete change* but rather prompts individuals to reflect on aspects they had previously ignored.

During an interview with architect Vittorio Gregotti about the controversial Zen of Palermo he designed, when asked if he could to live in that structure, his response was: *The conditions are not there: I cannot live in Zen, I am not a laborer, I do other things, completely different ones.* These words can obviously be interpreted on a *human* level with negative judgment; yet, from a broader and more objective perspective, they clearly illustrate the influence individualism has on one's personality and in relation to the role one holds. The detachment created between the self and others is evident and leads to a distinct selection of choices when relating to what is perceived as *external* or *internal* to the personal sphere.

Therefore, the *limit* that must be faced and overcome is not related to the *knowledge* individuals possess, but rather to how they use it to evolve and interact with others. In addition, as mentioned before, it is worth recalling that famous saying used in many religious and philosophical traditions: *Do to others as you would have them do to you*. Whether as a trainer or a leader, one's actions should be guided by this principle, putting oneself in others' shoes and interacting with them through those qualities that refer to one's personality and the way of observing others.

Chapter 7

Communication: The Starting Point to change the Narrative of the surrounding World

Communication is the spark that ignites change, the starting point for rewriting the narrative of the world around us. What is the main element that unites human interactions? What characterizes training? From which *aspect* does the preparation and implementation of a leadership or competency development strategy begin? What is the primary characteristic present in research and experimentation that points the way to new knowledge? How trite it may sound, there is a fundamental component in these processes that *influence*, depending on how it is used, every aspect of people's existence and, despite the *social media* generation that defines modern society, not everyone can manage it: this is obviously *communication*. But what does it *really* mean to communicate?

From an etymological perspective, to *communicate* means to *share* or *pool*, a sign or meaning that assumes a shared dimension. People communicate at work, in their free time, and with family; while they train and are trained; while they examine and are examined;

when they desire something and plan the path to obtain it, and so on. According to Watzlawick, Beavin, and Jackson, individuals are always *communicating*, even when they do not use *spoken* language: *metacommunication*, in fact, involves the body, facial expressions, and tone of voice; it is not as easy to control as spoken words and often reveals the true emotions and intentions of an individual[16].

In people's life, communication is one of the essential skills used and developed to interact with the outside world: in newborns, it manifests through crying to seek satisfaction of the basic needs, while a smile or calmness show feelings of pleasure or contentment. At the same time, parents begin to *show* the child the world around them-the objects, the actions taking place in front of their eyes- and they associate them with the sounds of the words that represent them in the language the child will learn.

According to Frederic Skinner, for example, this process follows the rules of *reinforcement*: *words* are seen as *labels* attached to objects that the child learns based on feedback from adults. In contrast, Noam

---

[16] Watzlawick, P., Beavin, J.H., Jackson, D.D. (1967). *Pragmatics of Human Communication: A Study of Interactional Patterns, Pathologies, and Paradoxes*. New York, London: W. W. Norton & Company, Inc.

Chomsky's *psycholinguistic* approach suggests that humans are born with an *innate* neural system that guides language learning with its own structural characteristics. Naturally, as individuals grow, they also assimilate meanings related to the *semantics* and *pragmatics* of communication, assigning *meanings* that go beyond the literal or denotative meanings found in dictionaries or reference texts, and instead relate to the *context* in which words are used and the *culture* in which individuals grow and develop.

To give a concrete example, the word *color* takes on different meanings in some cultures compared to others. In many Western cultures, color is often associated with visual perception and the light reflected by objects. However, in other cultures, such as those of Native Americans or certain African tribes, the concept of color may carry broader, deeper meanings connected to spirituality, nature, and the connection with the surrounding world: more specifically, in some Native American tribes, colors may represent the four cardinal directions, natural elements, or different life stages. Therefore, while the term *color* may seem similar across various cultures, its meaning and importance can vary greatly.

Yet, for a communication process to be *effective*, the participants must respect certain important rules that allow them to complete it. In fact, the meaning of *communication* is often confusing with that of simply *talking*, completely missing the primary goal of this action. Communication is not the *imposition* of a message between a sender and a receiver but, on the contrary, it should be an *equal* exchange of information leading to a goal.

In fact, those who assume the role of receiver in a conversation should engage in two types of efforts: the first involves processing the meaning of the message received through cognitive processes tied to their knowledge, cultural background, and experiences.

Then, the second effort should be to provide an appropriate *response* in the form of *feedback*: a process that should characterize every communicative context, from debates to clarifying tasks, from training to sharing an idea or opinion, and so on. This *role* reversal should continue until the communication is concluded, which does not necessarily mean that the of the original purpose for which it began is achieved.

Indeed, another aspect that is often overlooked, affecting both this area and all other human interactions, is the awareness and motivations of individuals in these circumstances: if they are not *aligned*, they will not be able to process the information received on an equal footing, nor will they have the *willingness* to see reality from the other's perspective to achieve a common result. This complexity is almost never considered until, as can also be highlighted in the stories previously mentioned by the interviewed trainers, it manifests in the failure of the communication efforts made. To give a simple example, it would be like a physicist giving a lecture on quantum physics at a gardening conference. No matter how clear and detailed the message may seem, it would fail to be understood by those with whom they are conversing.

An interesting approach in this regard is that of Deirdre Wilson and Dan Sperber on the *theory of relevance*: a speaker's statements carry *expectations* of relevance sufficient for the listener to understand what the speaker is trying to communicate. These expectations arise from the relationship an individual has with the other person, the role they play, and the type of interpretation being employed: the more *relevant* information, the less cognitive *effort* is required to perceive and understand it[17].

---

[17] Sperber, D. & Wilson, D. (1986/95a). *Relevance: Communication and Cognition*. Oxford: Blackwell. Second edition 1995.

People, therefore, tend to choose *stimuli* they find most relevant to either confirm or modify their representation of the world around them. To use the same examples as before, when a leader, a human resources specialist, or a trainer *interacts* with employees or trainees, they *offer* suggestions, theories, and strategies they have *learned* and *understood* during their professional or academic journeys: they do not represent an *absolute* reality but rather *interpretations* of a part of it. Yet, as often happens, if these interventions are not *relevant* to the needs of those with whom they are interacting, they will appear like misunderstood metaphors that may even generate opposite effects of those desired.

This communicative process, like others, often lacks a component that many mistakenly believe they respect but frequently neglect: the ability to *listen*. Truly paying attention to what is being said - being present both physically and cognitively - is not as simple as it may appear: being distracted during a conversation could result in the loss of useful information needed to provide an appropriate response, but it also indicates a disinterest in what is being communicated, which may be perceived by the speaker, particularly through the aforementioned metacommunication. This can demotivate the speaker, causing them to lose trust in their interlocutor.

Julian Treasure introduced the concept of *conscious listening* and developed several strategies and techniques to improve people's listening abilities. In his work, he emphasizes the importance of being fully present and focused during the act of listening, avoiding distractions, and practicing empathy and understanding toward others. This concept echoes earlier studies by Carl Rogers on client-centered therapy and the development of a fundamental technique related to *empathic listening*.

According to the American psychologist, empathic listening involves the ability to deeply and accurately understand what the other person is expressing, without judgment or interpretation. This type of listening implies the ability to put oneself in the other's shoes, to perceive and reflect the emotions, feelings, and implicit meanings in the message conveyed by the person they are conversing with. Rogers believed that empathic listening was essential to establish a climate of trust and understanding in therapeutic relationships and also in everyday interpersonal relationships. His ideas on listening and empathy have had a significant impact not only in the field of psychotherapy but also in areas such as communication, leadership, and counseling[18].

Additionally, experiencing difficulties in maintaining a certain detachment from one's *emotions* on the topics being communicated - especially in relation to the personal *experiences* that everyone brings to their daily actions - could result in an incongruent *response* to the conversation or an abrupt end to the communication process before achieving the desired outcome.

For example, Daryl Davis, an American R&B and blues musician and activist, became famous for his fight against racism and the controversial way he pursued it. In the early 1980s, after a performance at a venue, a man approached him to compliment his singing. To Davis's great surprise, the man revealed that he was an active member of the Ku Klux Klan (KKK). From this event, a friendship was born and allowed Devis to get to know this group and its members better: through dialogue, Davis convinced dozens of Klansmen to leave the organization and even denounce its members. The *extraordinary* and yet unmentioned aspect of this story is the fact that Daryl Davis is African American. Communicating and listening appropriately can make a difference, even in

---

[18] Rogers, Carl. (1951). *Client-Centered Therapy: Its Current Practice, Implications and Theory*. London: Constable.

tremendously complicated situations like the one just described.

In the workplace, as in training contexts, deepening our understanding of people and their needs can make all the difference in achieving the changes necessary to reach goals that, nowadays, are less related to *visible* and *practical* aspects of organizations and more to the intrinsic relationships that are cultivated within them. Nevertheless, changing the mental constructs that a person has built throughout their life is not easy, although it is not as difficult as it may seem.

In this regard, it is worth mentioning Jean Piaget's theory of learning, which is closely tied to the cognitive abilities of the individuals involved. According to the Swiss psychologist and educator, the force that drives a person to form increasingly complex and organized mental structures throughout cognitive development is the *factor of equilibrium*, which is an intrinsic and constitutive property of organic and mental life. Development, therefore, has an individual origin, and external factors such as the environment and social interactions may facilitate it, but they are not its cause. Piaget argued that the two processes characterizing adaptation are *assimilation* and *accommodation*, which alternate throughout the entire development process: both processes follow the entire cognitive journey of an individual, flexible and plastic in youth, more rigid with age, and are closely related to the concept of training repeatedly mentioned.

The first, assimilation, involves incorporating an event or object into a behavioral or cognitive schema that has already been acquired, while accommodation involves modifying the cognitive structure or behavioral schema to integrate new objects or events that were previously unknown. The two processes alternate in the constant search for a fluctuating balance (*homeostasis*), a form of control over the external world. When new information cannot be immediately interpreted based on existing schemas, the individual enters a state of disequilibrium and seeks to find a new cognitive balance, either by modifying their cognitive schemas to incorporate the newly acquired knowledge or discarding the information considered *negligible*.

Changing communication schemas on multiple levels - from social to professional - is the key to developing everything else, whether it be performing a task, forming an opinion on a behavior, developing a new idea, engaging in dialogue to clarify positions, or addressing issues related to advancement policies and training practices, among other areas of interaction between individuals. Adopting an effective and ethical communication method should be the starting point for building a healthy and ethical organizational culture: creating, therefore, a new narrative that fosters new beliefs, values, and methodologies to replace the obsolete and counterproductive ones that continue to persist in everyday practices and behaviors.

In early communication theories of the 1960s, John Langshaw Austin defined one of the *three speech acts* as the one that is *performed by saying something*, representing the effect that communication has on the reality surrounding individuals. *Language* describes the beliefs, values, and customs of a society; at the same time, when change occurs, the communicative process outlines not only the new social traits but also transforms the narrative that makes the future society real.

Indeed, the ultimate sense of communication, according to Jerome Bruner, is the *narrative* that structures reality and through which humans confer meaning to their experiences, outlining interpretative and prefigurative coordinates of events, actions, and situations that help build forms of knowledge to guide future interventions[19].

Therefore, *narrative thinking* is particularly effective in clarifying and understanding events, experiences, and human situations characterized by strong intentionality, as well as in focusing on complex units of analysis where human subjects, their stories, cultural and ethical choices, motivations, and intersubjective relationships play a central role. These aspects are critical on both *cognitive/cultural* and *emotional/relational* levels.

In *clinical practice*, as in everyday life, both psychologists and patients gain access to *autobiographical memories* through language and narration. The ability to narrate, understood as a mental function, is essential for organizing one's inner world and assigning meaning to human experience. For this reason, it is highly functional for understanding the various forms of human behavior and the knowledge that emerges from it. Thus, human existence is constantly subject to deconstructive and reconstructive processes, from which new and

---

[19] Bruner J. (1986). *Actual minds, possible words*. Cambridge: Harvard University Press.

different knowledge elements emerge that will guide an individual's behavior and decisions.

Therefore, before searching for a theory to explain, a strategy to apply, or motivations to stimulate, it is necessary to change the narrative by which people perceive work. This does not require complex philosophical dissertations, but rather a reappropriation of that *ethics* and *respect* this world, perhaps, has never fully integrated, because work was formerly perceived as something reserved for the lowest classes or, as in the modern context, is confined within the simple performance-payment negotiations, framing all those social interactions that, on the contrary, cannot be *confined* within regulations or forms of reward.

At the same time, attempting to classify a few aspects and include them in a course to explain to a group of people what is wrong in their work environment is useless and, perhaps, unconvincing. Training in the workplace cannot be interpreted as a *generic*, one-size-fits-all process, regardless of the background and expectations that an individual brings. This approach has not worked in the past and is still not effective today, for practical solutions tailored to specific situations are required.

Work can no longer be understood through *negative* or *utilitarian* connotations, as it has often been described. Instead, it must be seen as a *tool* to create well-being, both in the results it produces and in the fulfillment of the professional and personal needs of those who engage in it: this is because work is regulated not only by the practical act of exercising one's profession but also by the network of relationships established between individuals capable of thinking and feeling; thus, it should be considered and managed accordingly.

Communication, however difficult to implement, is the only tool that allows people to clarify perspectives and aspirations, resolve dilemmas and controversies, and bring to *life* what has so far only been reported in books or applied in a limited number of organizations. Communication is the starting point for initiating that process of reform that balances work with private life.

However, abandoning the *egocentric* and *generalized* approach that has been pursued so far to improve working conditions, professional relationships, group management, and training is seen as an impossible *utopia*, precisely because of the perception of the *effort* that each individual would need to make to analyze and intervene in this regarding: yet, underlying these fears is the *unconscious* awareness of the need to restructure oneself, one's beliefs, needs, and goals, to move from an *individualistic*, seemingly *easier* vision, to an *altruistic*, and perhaps more *complex*, one.

In fact, the discomfort experienced in today's workplace, which reflects the society we live in, is tied to primitive *survival* instincts that the modern world can no longer rely on. The gap between past workplace strategies and the cognitive development of individuals can no longer be ignored and must be taken into account when evaluating how to act in this regard: using coercion, mere economic incentives, or the frequently mentioned "*pat on the back*" to *motivate* people to work is no longer sufficient and, on the contrary, often leads to the opposite result.

This process also involves another aspect of communication that many people today tend to avoid, especially due to personal characteristics and the influence of *political correctness* mentioned earlier: *confrontation*. Knowing that exchanging certain opinions or ideas might lead to *conflict* with other group members makes many individuals uncomfortable, especially in critical circumstances where both personal and company interests are at stake. Just think of situations where an employee suffers injustice from a superior, or when colleagues have opposing points of views on how to perform a certain task: avoiding such disputes may bring temporary *relief* for having sidestepped the discussion, but over time, it risks becoming a source of personal *discomfort*, at both a psychological level and a physiological level.

Yet, to understand how difficult it is to face any conflict situation, even in North American ice hockey teams, where the physical build of many players is evidently *robust*, there are actual *roles* for those who, often technically mediocre, serves as *bodyguards* for other players or act with the sole intent of provoking a fight with the opposing team: in fact, physical altercations in this sport are semi-organized fights, governed by an informal code of honor, with players known as *enforcers*, whose task is to provoke and carry them out.

In the world of *negotiations*, which obviously includes all economic, political, labor, and union realities where conflict arises between two or more parties aiming to reach an agreement, the players called upon to secure a favorable outcome are known as *mediators*: of course, the context is not the same as the aforementioned sport, but verbal *confrontations* can assume similar criticality and make the difference between a *favorable* or *unfavorable* result for a given party.

These two examples, despite being at diametrically opposite poles, can serve on the one hand, to understand the physical and psychological difficulties an individual must face before, during, and after a confrontation, and, on the other, to highlight its importance. Yet, within organizations, this *culture of confrontation* - i.e. the practice of clarifying the positions opposing the common thinking and action of the working group or the managers themselves - is missing. For decades, studies on *feedback* and its value have been conducted, suggesting how to *regulate* and *control* this flow of interventions.

As early as 1868, James Maxwell, in publishing a study on automatic systems, used the term *positive* for those systems in which feedback represented continuous change, and *negative* for feedback in which the functioning remained unchanged. In the mid-20th century, within mechanical approaches to communication, Norbert Wiener considered feedback as the *verbal* or *non-verbal* message returned from the receiver to the sender, which was a function of the level of listening and attention given to the received message.

In today's work context, feedback is seen as a tool to improve results necessary to achieve specific goals, but it is the individual's *awareness* that determines its interpretation and, therefore, its success or failure. In fact, it is through confrontation with the external world that an individual can develop and learn to recognize their role and relationship with others: confrontation is the opportunity to understand one's own and others' needs, to activate appropriate behaviors in a given context, correct mistakes, and come into contact with their own limitations.

Through confrontation it is possible to explore all available *opportunities* to emerge from the routines to which an individual and the work environment are anchored and, thus, open up to new lines of thought, new ways of learning and improving. However, the issue that companies, leaders, and workgroups must resolve is overcoming the interpretative obstacle of *confrontation communication*, which today is linked to the perception of discomfort, inadequacy, and fear, and which hinders the very opportunity for development, personal growth, and civilization that many studies have shown is achievable.

And this process, like the entire *concept* of work, can only begin by *reconceptualizing* the narrative currently in use, which represents an obsolete past. In fact, there are still people who, when *observing* today's work situation, refuse to talk about complete *dissatisfaction* when referring to the *problems* related to the world of work and how to attempt to solve them. And they are not entirely wrong: when comparing modern times to just two centuries ago, it is clear that many aspects have improved, both in terms of working conditions and the situations in which employees operate, as well as in economic terms, and consequently in terms of the well-being achieved. Nonetheless, recalling that *optimistic/pessimistic* definition of the *half full/half empty glass*, this *half well-being*—or *half discomfort*, depending on the perspective—still lacks a half that, given the level of knowledge and awareness reached today, is *theoretically* easily achievable.

Yet, it is from the narrative currently in use that *comparisons* like these arise and that *validate* assumptions such as the one previously mentioned - namely, that it is *normal* to experience certain discomforts at work since it cannot be considered a pastime. Therefore, it is by adopting a new *narrative* about this reality, along with promoting procedures, behaviors, and personal profiles within it, that change can happen and the *balance* between private life and work that is currently lacking, and which has been implied by the results of studies conducted to this day, can be achieved: becoming aware of the fact that companies and employees have much in common, especially their *well-being*, and that this can only improve through close *collaboration* , built on *respect*, *ethics*, and *trust* between these two key players. This should be the foundation upon which all organizational cultures should be based, to create a work environment that *protects* its members from mismanagement or individuals who undermine its stability.

In this way, people can *reclaim* their time, as well as the physical and mental state necessary to take care of themselves, their families, their children, and their relationships with others - things they are currently unable to manage properly due to the conditions in which they work. This lack of balance impacts not only on their own well-being but also that of their loved ones, the companies they work for, and even the issues that today's world increasingly struggles to address.

This is a period of transition, and it is undeniable. The studies conducted so far across all humanistic fields prove that society still has much work to do in order to bring about the changes needed to improve people's lives: however, it is only through awareness and the reshaping of the existing narrative frameworks that we can achieve a balance between theoretical knowledge and its application to reality.

Of course, many questions remain unanswered, particularly on the *macro socio-cultural level*, but one question might give readers of this book an idea of where they stand at this historical moment, both in terms of awareness and personal preparation: Do I possess the will to pursue a path of sacrifices and uncertainties to change what I know, myself, and my way of observing the world, or do I prefer to remain loyal to the customs in which I have been developed and leave this task to others? Because change, above all, starts with being able to change oneself before attempting to change the world around us.

Bibliography

1) Geoffrey Barraclough, *Guida alla storia contemporanea* - Ed. Laterza, 2004.

2) *Wilhelm Wundt*. Trovato il 22 Luglio 2024 su *Enciclopedia Britannica*. Enciclopedia Britannica, Inc.

3) Hugo Münsterberg. Trovato il 22 Luglio 2024 su *Enciclopedia Britannica*. Enciclopedia Britannica, Inc.

4) Mayo, E. (1933). *The Human Problems of an Industrial Civilization*. New York: The Macmillan Company.

5) Session: "Psychological Safety at Work" (https://www.linkedin.com/events/6986336540587126785/comments/ - min 45:11)".

6) Bronfenbrenner, U. (1979). *The Ecology of Human Development*. Cambridge, Massachusetts, and London, England: Harvard University Press.

7) Bronfenbrenner, U. (2004). *Making Human Beings Human*. Cornell University: Sage Publication.

8) Maslow, A. H. (1943). A theory of human motivation. *Psychological Review*. 50(4), 370–396.

9) Hersey, P. Blanchard, K. (1969). *Management of Organizational Behavior: Utilizing Human Resources.* Englewood Cliffs, New Jersey: Prentice Hall.

10) Hein, H. (2009) *Motivation: Motivationsteori og praktisk anvendelse.* Copenhagen: Hans Reitzels Forlag.

11) Freire, P. (2004). *Pedagogia dell'autonomia. Saperi necessari per la pratica educativa.* Torino: EGA.

12) Tajfel, H., Flament. C., Billig, M. G. & Bundy, R. P. (1971). Social categorization and intergroup behaviour. *European Journal of Social Psychology*, *1*, 149-178.

13) Tajfel, H. & Turner, J.C. (1979). *An integrative theory of intergroup conflict.* In W. G. Austin & S. Worchel (Eds), *The social psychology of intergroup relations.* (pp. 33-47). Monterey, CA: Brooks Cole.

14) Mowday, R.T., Sutton, R.I. (1993). Organizational behaviour: linking individuals and groups to organizational context. *Annual Review of Psychology*, 44, 195-229.

15) Turner, J.C., Hogg, M.A., Oakes, P.J., Reicher, S.D., Wetherell, M.S. (1987). *Rediscovering the social group: A self-categorization theory.* Cambridge, MA, US: Basil Blackwell.

16) Watzlawick, P., Beavin, J.H., Jackson, D.D. (1967). *Pragmatics of Human Communication: A Study of Interactional Patterns, Pathologies, and Paradoxes*. New York, London: W. W. Norton & Company, Inc.

17) Sperber, D. & Wilson, D. (1986/95a). *Relevance: Communication and Cognition*. Oxford: Blackwell. Second edition 1995.

18) Rogers, Carl. (1951). *Client-Centered Therapy: Its Current Practice, Implications and Theory*. London: Constable.

19) Bruner J. (1986). *Actual minds, possible words*. Cambridge: Harvard University Press.

www.ingramcontent.com/pod-product-compliance
Lightning Source LLC
Chambersburg PA
CBHW070157230526
45471CB00002B/701